A STEP-BY-STEP BOOK ABOUT
TRAINING YOUR PARAKEET

J. DARLENE CAMPBELL

Photography: H. Bielfeld, Darlene Campbell, Penny Corbett and Stephanie Logue, Garry Duesler, Michael Gilroy, Keith Hindwood, Harry V. Lacey, Louise Van der Meid, Ron and Val Moat, Vince Serbin, and Norma Veitch. Humorous drawings by Andrew Prendimano.

Distributed in the UNITED STATES by T.F.H. Publications, Inc., One T.F.H. Plaza, Neptune City, NJ 07753; in CANADA to the Pet Trade by H & L Pet Supplies Inc., 27 Kingston Crescent, Kitchener, Ontario N2B 2T6; Rolf C. Hagen Ltd., 3225 Sartelon Street, Montreal 382 Quebec; in CANADA to the Book Trade by Macmillan of Canada (A Division of Canada Publishing Corporation), 164 Commander Boulevard, Agincourt, Ontario M1S 3C7; in ENGLAND by T.F.H. Publications Limited, Cliveden House/Priors Way/Bray, Maidenhead, Berkshire SL6 2HP, England; in AUSTRALIA AND THE SOUTH PACIFIC by T.F.H. (Australia) Pty. Ltd., Box 149, Brookvale 2100 N.S.W., Australia; in NEW ZEALAND by Ross Haines & Son, Ltd., 82 D Elizabeth Knox Place, Panmure, Auckland, New Zealand; in the PHILIPPINES by Bio-Research, 5 Lippay Street, San Lorenzo Village, Makati Rizal; in SOUTH AFRICA by Multipet Pty. Ltd., Box 235, New Germany, South Africa 3620. Published by T.F.H. Publications, Inc. Manufactured in the United States of America by T.F.H. Publications, Inc.

CONTENTS

HISTORY

The brightly colored parakeet, one of the most popular pets in America, originates from Australia. In his native land the parakeet groups with thousands of his own kind in great migratory flocks. The flock follows water-courses and lives off wild grasses, seeds and the scrub vegetation of the dry grasslands.

Another name for parakeet is *Budgerigar*, which is an English translation of the bushman's name for the colorful bird, *Betcherrygar*. The aborigines of Australia did not tame the beautiful birds; they ate them. Betcherrygar, roughly translated, means "pretty good eating."

The term parakeet is an English form of the French word *Paroquette*, meaning "little parrot." Add to that such terms as Undulated, or Shell Parakeet, and you describe the bird's markings such as a striped or sea-shell pattern of black across its head, neck and wings.

The parakeet did not always know such favoritism in America, however. It was not until 1840 that the spunky little bird began to find popularity. It was through the British naturalist, John Gould, that the parakeet arrived in England. John Gould was doing a study in Australia and brought a number of live birds back to England upon his return. The little birds proved to be a great curiosity.

Gould's brother-in-law took such an interest in the birds that he began breeding them. The popularity of the bird grew so rapidly that soon they were in great demand across England.

For some unknown reason, Holland and Belgium became centers for parakeet breeding. The budgie, short for Budgerigar, was introduced to Germany in 1855. Grafin von Schwerin introduced them and began breeding them as a

FACING PAGE: Budgerigars are able, intelligent, affordable pets found throughout the world.

4

This good-size, radiant parakeet is referred to as a yellow-face opaline mauve; note the proud stance of this bird.

hobby. Again, the popularity of the little bird grew, and a demand sprang up in Germany.

Today parakeets are found in all parts of the world. They are in all pet shops and pet departments of large variety stores in America. One reason for this popularity is that the bird breeds readily in captivity, allowing the price to remain within the average pet buyer's limits. Another item in favor of the parakeet is its intelligence and ability to learn tricks quickly. A natural mimic, the bird easily learns to talk by mimicking the human voice.

One of the attractive points of budgerigars is their wide range of available colors; note the difference between this violet cinnamon and the yellow-face above.

These bright-eyed and alert budgerigars show just two of the many color varieties of budgies. The many color variations and the endless possibilities afforded by careful breeding for type and color are two very appealing assets found in the popular "little parrot."

SELECTION

When shopping for a bird, the wisest choice in selecting a pet is to start with a young one. The phrase, "You can't teach an old dog new tricks" has been disproven, for when it comes to older parakeets it usually takes a little more time and little more patience in training but they can be finger tamed and may even learn to talk. Older birds tend to become set in their ways and stubbornly refuse to change acquired habits or to add new ones, but if training is fun for the bird, it can be taught.

Of course, the younger the bird you purchase, the better your chances of it attaching its affections to you instead of to another bird. Also, it is best to keep only one bird as a pet if you want to teach it to talk. With no other bird for a companion, the parakeet will be easier to tame and to train. Being a playful bird, the lone parakeet will seek you out as a playmate. If you are away from home most of the time and feel the bird will be lonely and you do not have the time to devote to training, then a pair of parakeets will keep each other amused and happy.

Generally speaking, males make the better talkers. It is difficult to tell the difference between the male and the female parakeet when they are young, but it can be done. No matter what the color of the bird, in the adult male the cere, or the dark bridge across the upper part of the beak, is a dark blue. In the female the cere remains white, pink, brown, or pale blue. Baby birds of both sexes have a light blue cere, so it is with difficulty that the sex can be distinguished. When in doubt, ask the person selling the birds to distinguish the sex for you.

FACING PAGE: A fully darkened eye is a key used in selecting a young bird; the iris of this eye is beginning to lighten, suggesting an age of about three months.

Older birds may initially be less friendly; they may also have a painful bite.

It is best to start with a young bird of less than three months of age. He will be easy to tame and train, and it is easier to tell the age of a young bird than the sex. The easiest way to tell a young bird from an older one is by the shell-like stripes which cover the head and neck. These stripes run all the way to the beak, and as the young bird matures they gradually disappear. The cap becomes white on the blue-colored birds, and yellow on the green and yellow birds. The change begins to take place at the age of ten to twelve weeks of age.

Another sign to look for when selecting a young bird is found in the eyes. A baby parakeet's eyes appear larger than the eyes of older birds. This is due to the fact that both the iris and the pupil are a solid black. At about three months of age, the iris begins to lighten in color. By the time the bird is fully grown, the iris is gray while the pupil remains dark black. This gives the appearance of a small black eye encircled with a gray ring.

When examining a group of birds in a pet shop, look then for the youngest bird by the stripes on the head, the solid black eyes, and the light-colored cere. This will assure you of getting a bird that is young enough to train.

While looking for a baby bird, it cannot be stressed enough the importance of selecting a healthy one. Too often a

person is attracted to a particular color of bird without regard to the condition of the feathers or the bird's constitution. When a bird dies a few days after it is taken home, it leads to disappointment and the misconception that the parakeet is a difficult bird to raise. Nothing is further from the truth.

Parakeets are known to live long lives, the average being eight to ten years under varied conditions, whether it be in a large farm house or small city apartment. Some individuals have been known to live as long as fifteen to twenty years. Start with a healthy bird and you will have a pet that will live for years, providing you give it proper care.

The first sign of an unthrifty bird is shown in its feathers. If it sits quietly with its feathers all puffed up, the bird is not well. Stained or missing feathers around the vent are an indication of diarrhea. Avoid the bird that sits sluggishly with its wings drooped, has a short or damaged tail, or is dull and unresponsive.

The healthy bird sits alertly, reacts to movements, flies about the cage or is active on the perch. It may try for attention from other birds within the cage, or it may amuse itself by picking at objects within the cage. It uses its beak to climb with, to preen its feathers with, and to investigate objects or other birds. In short, it is alert and active.

Equally important as the selection of a healthy bird is the maintenance of the bird's health after purchase. A ''Jungle-Gym'' (shown below) or other exercise system especially designed to be of interest to your budgie will stimulate its desire to exercise.

HOUSING

The main consideration in selecting a cage for your parakeet is to be sure to purchase one that is large enough. Cages come in all price ranges, from the modestly priced simple cage to exotic bird homes made of bamboo and having several tiers. Your parakeet will not notice your extravagance or the luxury of the cage, but it will notice the size. There is no such thing as a cage that is too large for a parakeet, but many are too small.

Cages with only vertical wires should be avoided, as the parakeet enjoys climbing up the sides. The lack of a cross wire will make it difficult, if not impossible, to perform this feat. Also, the wires should be spaced close enough so that the bird's head cannot pass through. Widely spaced wires are dangerous, as the bird may become caught and hang helplessly. A well-constructed cage will have cross wires running horizontally as well as vertical wires that are spaced evenly for the protection and safety of the bird.

A cage with a sliding tray floor makes cleaning easy. Also, some cages have wire bottoms above the tray. This is not as desirable as one that has the tray above the solid bottom of the cage. The parakeet likes to walk on the cage bottom and pick at grit spread there for the purpose, and with a wire bottom this is not possible.

To avoid the messy scattering of seed, the cage should also be equipped on all four sides with fine wire screening or a plastic barrier. The barrier should extend for a distance of several inches above the bottom. The barrier is removable for easy cleaning and changing of seed and water cups.

Facing Page: Budgerigars are easy to care for. They do require exercise, however, so keep in mind that a larger cage is often better because it allows more freedom of movement.

Preferred materials for cages are chrome or stainless steel, as they are easy to clean and never need painting. Painted metals are a good choice, but they tend to lose their paint in time as the bird picks at the bars. These cages can be repainted satisfactorily, giving many years of service.

To repaint an old cage, select a paint that is not lead base, as lead is fatal to birds. A parakeet will ingest small amounts of paint daily as it picks at the bars, and in time the lead which accumulates within the body will prove deadly. Oil-

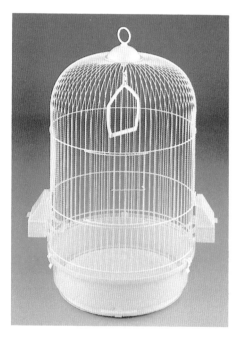

Hagen Products manufactures a variety of cage styles and colors that will easily match the decor of one's home as well as meet the needs of the bird.

base paints also are to be avoided. A quality latex-base paint will do the trick, and if you select a color to complement the room, you are adding a decorator touch.

Wood, bamboo, or wicker cages are to be avoided if possible. The parakeet will pick at the fibers and eventually the cage will have a ragged look. Also, these cages, being of natural materials, can harbor mites and lice in the cracks and crevices. They are difficult to clean.

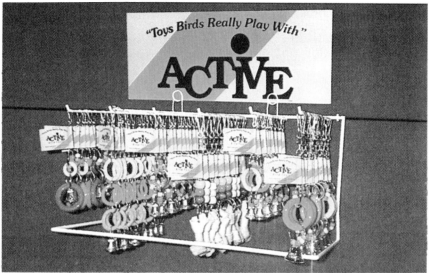

An assortment of toys can be found on display at your local pet store. Toys help to make the time your budgie spends in its cage fun and enjoyable. There are many different colors and styles to choose from. Be sure the toy you decide upon for your budgie is not too large. Ask the clerk in your pet store to recommend what may be best for your bird. Photo courtesy of Active Bird Toys.

The cage should be equipped with a seed cup, a water cup, and at least two perches. A good perch is of natural unfinished wood. The size of the perch should be about the same circumference as an adult person's finger. Doweling may be used, but never use a perch that has been painted, as the paint may prove toxic.

A swing is not necessary, but your parakeet will appreciate the hours of fun it offers. Most parakeets enjoy playing with the swing more than actually swinging on it. There are other playthings your bird will enjoy, but remember not to clutter the cage with too many items, as he will not have room to move about.

In the wilds the parakeet is bathed naturally by rain showers. In captivity, some birds may not be especially fond of water, or for some reason they have a dislike of the type of bath dish offered or have some other aversion to bathing. If your parakeet is one of these shy individuals that refuse to bathe, it is a simple matter to gently sprinkle him with water or to mist him with water from a spray bottle and then let him preen his feathers.

BATHING

The budgie is naturally clean and is capable of keeping himself that way without the aid of water. The constant preening of the feathers, the collecting of oil from a gland at the base of the tail and spreading it over each feather, will keep him well groomed.

Because they are naturally clean, they never need a real bath. That is to say, one never washes the bird with soap or other cleaning products which may prove toxic. However, the budgie may like to bathe regularly in his own manner. Everyday bathing is not necessary, but two or three times a week is desirable. A bath for a caged bird is a plastic device that fastens to the open door of the cage. The bird will learn to hop into the bath and do a lot of splashing. Then he will hop to a perch and spend much time preening his feathers.

A second method of bathing the bird is to place a shallow dish of tepid water on a table top. Be sure the table is covered with a sheet of plastic or other material to protect the surface from water. Remove the bottom of the cage and place the cage over the dish of water on the table. The bird will discover the dish and hop into it, and with much splashing and fluttering, take a bath.

Facing page: Parakeets (and other parrots) are excellent climbers and can easily perch on narrow rims occasionally.

Be sure to remove feed cups before the bath begins, or the seed may get wet and spoiled.

As important as a clean bird is a clean cage. Your parakeet is clean by nature, and you should help him to keep clean; this includes housekeeping. It will take only a few minutes every few days to clean and freshen the cage to ensure your bird's health and comfort. Change the paper that lines the cage bottom, place fresh grit on the paper, change the feed and give fresh water.

A bird bath should be made available to your bird. This bird bath attaches easily to the door opening and therefore does not lessen the space inside the cage for the bird. Photo courtesy of Hagen Products.

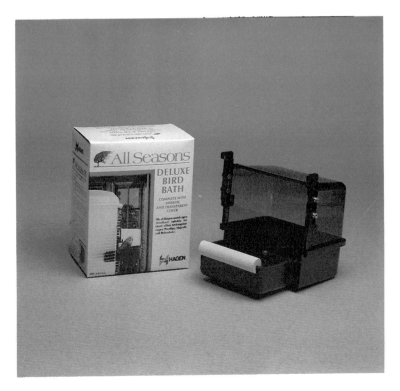

Budgies prefer to bathe under a water drip.

Occasionally a thorough cleaning is in order. This means wiping the perches and bars, scraping any accumulated droppings from the corners, and doing a good cleaning and disinfecting job.

It takes only a few minutes to clean the cage, and a few minutes more to do a thorough disinfecting job to prevent illness and parasites.

FEEDING

Feeding the parakeet is a simple matter. The manufacturers of bird products have combined the parakeet's natural diet in just the right amount so there is no guesswork in trying to add a variety of seeds. The basic diet is a mixture of canary seed and millet mixed, 60 percent canary seed to 40 percent millet for a young bird. As the bird grows older, a 50-50 mixture is ideal. Always buy *parakeet* seed and not canary seed. Buy in small quantities so that it stays fresh to the last feeding.

The parakeet will shell his seed and can fool you into thinking there is plenty of seed in his dish when actually it is full of hulls. To be sure your bird has adequate seed at all times and not merely hulls that he cannot eat, each day remove his seed cup from the cage, and hold it over a trash can or step outside, then blow lightly over the top. The hulls will be blown away, leaving the unshelled seed. Shake the cup and blow over it again to be sure of blowing all the chaff away. Now refill the cup with fresh seed and place it back in his cage.

Other items you will want to add for the health of the bird are cuttlebone, grit, a grit cup, and a bath dish. Cuttlebone is a piece of cuttlefish bone that attaches to the inside of the cage. It provides needed salts, trace elements, and minerals, and also sharpens and trims the beak. Cuttlebone is necessary to good health, and every caged bird should have access to this mineral supplement. It is an aid in trimming the beak since the beak of parakeets continues to grow—as do his toe nails. It is necessary for the budgie to trim his beak, and he will work to keep his beak in proper shape.

FACING PAGE: This olive green budgerigar shows the strong, solid body of a well-fed bird. Its breast is full and its plumage radiant.

Grit or bird gravel is used by the gizzard to grind food. Since the parakeet has no teeth, it needs grit to grind the seed and make it digestible. Be sure to purchase gravel of the proper size for parakeets, and sprinkle it generously over the bottom of the cage. Also add a grit cup and keep it filled.

Sand is not satisfactory, as it is dusty and has no grinding action. When no grit or gravel is available, the bird will eat any rough material it can find, and most materials such as newspaper are harmful. Not only is the printer's ink poisonous, but the paper will pack in the intestines, and the bird, unable to pass it out, will meet a painful, slow death.

Heather, a lovely tri-colored parakeet, learned to open the door to her cage, and in so doing would escape and fly about the room. To protect her from the cats also sharing the home, her owner used a *twist-um,* a paper-coated thin wire, to secure the cage door. Heather developed a habit of working her beak to keep in shape on the twist-um. The end result was that she sheared the paper from the wire, ingesting it. After several months of replacing the sheared twist-um with a new one, and several months of Heather's ingesting the paper coating, the little bird died. Had her owner realized the threat of paper to his pet's health, he would have secured the cage door with a paper clip.

Honey Sticks are a relished treat for your budgie. Available at pet stores, they are nutritious and a great deal of fun for your bird. Photo courtesy of Hagen Products.

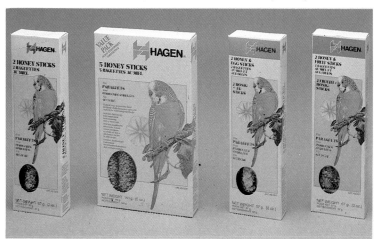

Greens are an important addition to the diet for their vitamin content and should be fed several times a week. These can be beet, carrot or celery tops, clover, parsley, or lettuce. You will also find a variety of suitable greens growing wild in your yard. Try offering grass, dandelion, plantain, foxtail, milk

Pet shops and bird specialty shops offer a wide variety of seed mixtures for all types of birds, all designed especially to suit the dietary requirements of the individual bird types. Photo courtesy of Pretty Bird International.

thistles and wild oats. If the bird's stools become loose, too many greens are being offered, so cut back on the amount. Parakeets are small birds, and it takes only a small amount of green vegetables and grasses to satisfy the need for extra nutrition.

Parakeets enjoy getting their own seeds, so place a small amount of lawn grass that has gone to seed in the cage, or some other wild grass in seed. Sometimes it is possible to

find at pet shops pots already planted with greens. Also, you can plant a teaspoon of bird seed in a small container and water it. It will sprout and, when placed inside the parakeet's cage, will give him a fresh supply of his own garden greens.

Be sure to wash greens that may have been sprayed with insecticides and pesticides, as these will cause illness. In large frequent doses they will cause an unexplained death.

An apple slice may be offered, but remove it if it is not eaten completely, for it will mold when left in the cage. Attach

This pair stops to enjoy a meal of fresh seed.

fresh greens to the inside of the cage with a clothes pin or paper clip.

Pet supply shops have a variety of treats available for budgies. Some of those available include various seed combinations, dried fruits and vegetables and sprays of millet. Spray millet is a natural treat of millet still on the stem. The bird enjoys picking his own seed from these sprays that hang in the cage. Honey sticks can be purchased, as can real fruit and vegetable treats with a few seeds included.

NYLABIRD® is specially designed to give your bird the calcium it needs while serving the practical purpose of a perch and dumbbell ring; thus, it saves money and possibly your bird's life.

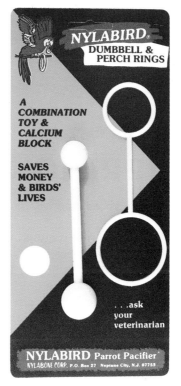

Treat cups can be purchased to add a supplement to the diet. These are seeds mixed with honey and packed tightly into a small cup that attaches to the side of the cage, giving the bird something to pick at. There are combination greens and grains already prepared and packaged for feeding. Greasy treats should never be offered, as the bird cannot digest them.

There are also various color conditioners, breeding foods, vitamins, and tonics available. When a good basic diet is supplied, these other items are not necessary, but they are fun to feed, and the bird enjoys them.

To insure against the tragic escape of your pet before he has had a chance to become acquainted with you, it is advisable to clip the wings. Wing clipping is painless, temporary, and aids in the taming and training of your parakeet.

CLIPPING

For the first clipping it is best to have two people do the procedure: one to hold the bird, the second to clip the wings. Once you have become experienced, you will be able to clip the wings without assistance.

The only tool required for this job is a sharp pair of household shears. Barber shears work fine, as do dressmaker shears. The important thing to remember is that the scissors you use be sharp so that a quick, clean cut is made and there is no damage to the wing or discomfort to the bird.

Learn the different feathers appearing on the wing. The large *primary* feathers correspond to our hands. The *secondary* feathers correspond to the bones of our forearms. It is the primary feathers that are the flight feathers, and it is these feathers that need clipping to prevent your budgie from flying away from you.

The center of each feather is a strong, stiff shaft. When fully grown, feathers have no nerves or blood supply. They are held tightly in sockets in the skin, and are shed during the period of *molt.* Molting occurs at least once a year, when new feathers replace the old ones as they fall out.

During the molting process, the new feathers contain tiny blood vessels which will bleed if cut into and cause pain. Clip the wings only after the feathers have reached their full growth and the blood supply is no longer present.

FACING PAGE: The owner gives his budgie its first wing clipping under the close supervision of an experienced friend. In this case, the primary feathers are being cut individually.

Exposing the primary feathers prior to clipping.

Have one person hold the bird securely in one hand and extend the wing with the other hand. It is not necessary to clip both wings, but many persons prefer both wings to be clipped, as this allows the bird to retain his natural balance. Using the shears, cut all the primary feathers.

A second type of cut is to remove all but two or three of the primaries, and also cut several secondaries. This is the preferred cut for the author. It gives a nice balanced look to the bird, preserves natural beauty of the main primaries, and at the same time, it prevents flight.

Clipping, especially unaided, requires experience.

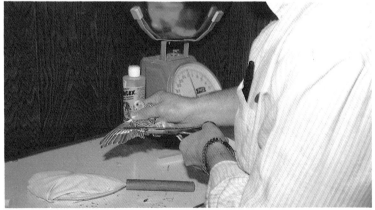

The right wing of this bird is fully clipped. Do not attempt to clip your bird's wings unless you have learned the proper method from an experienced professional.

Early training begins *inside* the cage. Finger training is the first lesson your parakeet will need to learn. It should begin within a few days after you bring your bird home. Do not let your pet out of his cage for at least one week after he has been introduced into your home. He needs this time to adjust and to feel secure in his new environment.

TAMING

To begin his training, slowly introduce a pencil about eight inches in length into his cage. Holding the pencil securely in one hand, move it slowly toward the bird. Introduce the pencil several times a day until he is no longer afraid of it.

The next step is to move the pencil slowly toward the bird and stroke his breast gently. Apply a gentle pressure up and back against his breast. When he allows you to do this, he will step up onto the pencil and perch there. Move the pencil slowly back and forth inside the cage with the bird perched on it. Repeat this trick several times a day for a day or two.

Your budgie is now ready to stand on your finger. Introduce your hand with a finger extended into the cage. Touch the bird's breast and apply gentle pressure up and back, the same as you did with the pencil. Your bird will step up onto your finger. Now move your hand slowly back and forth inside the cage with the bird sitting on it.

These training periods should be short and without distractions. Repeat them frequently throughout the day, speaking softly to accustom the parakeet to your voice. Only one person should attempt to train the bird so he will develop confidence in that person. Two or more persons will confuse him.

FACING PAGE: Either one of these young budgies would make a wonderful, highly trainable pet. To acquire a pet budgie, simply go to your local pet shop.

Once the bird has become used to sitting on your finger and will allow you to move him about within the cage, withdraw your hand slowly from the cage with the bird resting on your finger. Some birds will hop off the finger and back into the cage. Try again. Repeat this lesson over several days until you are successfully bringing the bird out of his cage to sit on your finger. Talk to him. Let him look at your lips as they move by bringing him up to your face.

As he becomes comfortable with this new phase of training, encourage him to step from one finger to the finger of the other hand by applying gentle pressure to his breast with that finger. Also encourage him to step to your shoulder or to the top of your head.

To get him to step to your shoulder, with the parakeet perched securely on your finger, bring your finger next to your shoulder. Roll your finger away with a slight twisting motion so that the parakeet will be forced to climb to your shoulder to retain a firm foothold.

Parakeets are responsive to a devoted owner and will soon learn to spend long periods of time in direct contact with people.

A pair of budgies will often be so interested in each other that neither will respond to training. If you want a tamed budgie, it is recommended that you keep individuals.

Budgies are responsive to a devoted owner and will soon learn to spend long periods of time riding on your shoulder or the top of your head. Older birds, too, can be finger trained and will enjoy riding on the shoulder, but it takes much more patience to win the confidence of an older bird.

Older birds have a very painful bite. When the bird bites, it rotates the mandibles from side to side in a very painful and prolonged grip. The bird can be forced to release its hold if you lightly thump its chin, or place your finger and thumb over the nostril holes in the beak. He will quickly release his hold to breathe. Never flick the beak or immerse the bird or its head in water to make it release its hold, as this may cause the budgie to develop a bad temperament. It is far better to be prepared. Until you have successfully trained the older bird that makes a habit of biting, wear tightly fitting leather gloves or wrap the

finger and thumb in masking tape. It only takes a time or two for the budgie to learn that his biting is to no avail and he will give up the habit.

Should your budgie become frightened and attempt to fly away during a training session, place him back in the security of his cage. Try training again later.

By now you and your bird are both feeling more comfortable with each other. You want to move ahead and teach things that are not in this book; by all means do so. You will discover the bird wants to learn too, that learning for the budgie is fun for him and entertainment for you.

Karen, the author's daughter, offers her pet a treat for being such an able student. Offering rewards for tasks well done is an enjoyable way to supplement your parakeet's diet.

The reason that budgies kept individually tame better than ones kept in pairs or groups is that budgies, like most all other birds, are monogamous—that is they choose one mate for life. With no other bird available for this selective affection, it is likely that your budgie will choose you as its "partner."

TALKING

All parrots and parrot-like birds can be taught to talk. Your parakeet is no exception. He is a great little mimic and will mimic your voice, the sounds he hears indoors, or wild birds he hears through an open window. If you want him to mimic your voice, he must be isolated from other birds and, again, you must be the only trainer he has or he will become confused.

The budgie, even though he learns to talk, does not actually understand the word he is repeating. He is imitating the sounds he hears, not real words. Generally, young males learn to imitate human speech more easily than females. But that does not mean that females cannot learn to talk. They are not as quick to learn to mimic the human voice, and their mimicking may not be as distinct as that of the male. To produce a good talker, start with a young male.

Pairs kept together almost never learn to talk; they are too interested in each other. That is why it was important from the beginning to win your budgie's confidence and his affection. You are now his sole interest and he will mimic your voice if you use repetition and patience. Repetition is the key. Choose a word that is simple, such as *hello* or *hi.* Repeat it clearly over and over from a short distance away.

My first parakeet refused to learn to mimic my voice when I was present. I gave up teaching him to talk until after he had learned to whistle. I began giving a wolf whistle every time I passed his cage. One day I was in another room when I heard Dicky Bird whistle. It was the wolf whistle I used each time I passed his cage. I whistled back from the room I was in, and he answered. From then on we kept up a whistling conversation. He seemed to whistle when he wanted attention from me.

FACING PAGE: Almost any parakeet can learn to mimic a human voice; patience and persistence are the keys to instruction.

Within a few weeks he was mimicking my calling the cat. At near the same time each evening, I would call the cat indoors to be fed. Dicky Bird began calling the cat, too.

Now I realized that Dicky Bird was mimicking me, but not what I wanted him to learn. He was picking up what he heard me repeat daily from other parts of the house. So I began teaching him from a separate room. I would lie on the bed in the bedroom with the door open to the other room where Dicky Bird was caged. Then I would repeat, loud enough so that he could hear, phrases like *Pretty Boy . . . Oh, boy . . . kiss me.*

Dicky Bird learned different phrases in succession, but he put them together in his own combination with the cat call and the wolf whistle. His own rendition came out like this, *wolf whistle!, kitty, kitty, kitty, oh boy, kiss me!* He never learned to say *pretty boy.* Perhaps he never met a pretty boy that he liked.

If you have neither the time nor the patience for training your bird to talk, there are records available at pet shops with phrases already recorded. Another popular device is the tape recorder. With an inexpensive tape recorder, you can record your first training session, then play the tape for successive sessions until your budgie has learned his first lesson in talking. Then you can change the word, words, or phrase on the tape for his next lesson.

The time it takes to train your parakeet to talk will depend on his willingness to learn. Some birds will respond in a week, while others take a year to learn the first word. Remember that you must have patience. Once your bird has learned to mimic your voice he will pick up the next word or phrase more quickly.

Maintain a uniform schedule for daily training sessions. One half hour of each day is sufficient. Once your bird has said his first word, encourage him to repeat it over and over until the pronunciation is clear. The first word is the most difficult, so continue working with your bird to say the word correctly for several days before moving on to the next word.

Once your pet has a vocabulary of 15 to 20 words, he will begin adding a few of his own, words you had no intention of teaching him.

TALKING

Some people claim they cannot understand the words parakeets mimic. This is due to a lazy trainer. When the bird first mimics, it is unclear and unrecognizable to all but the trainer who has worked so hard for so many hours. Now is the hour of success! The trainer feels jubilant. He can hardly wait to successfully teach another word. So it goes. The parakeet learns, but before he has learned the proper pronunciation he is off on another lesson to learn another word. The bird does not know he is not clearly repeating the word because the trainer is satisfied. And once the bird has the habit of repeating the word indistinctly, he will not change his manner of talk.

Continue to work with your bird until it is saying the word clearly before going on to the next word.

Recording your bird will enable you to listen closely to its pronunciation and to make the necessary corrections.

SICKNESS

If properly cared for, the parakeet will live out its life without illness. It is beyond the scope of this book to describe all manners of illnesses or to prescribe all manners of cures. As in all matters of health, an ounce of prevention is worth a pound of cure. A well cared for parakeet, one that is well fed, comfortably housed, and kept free from drafts and parasites, will not be prone to sickness. Parakeets are hardy birds, and the majority of health problems arise from accidents within the home while the bird is allowed to fly free.

ACCIDENTS: The number one cause of accidents is other pets. The most trusted dog or cat cannot be trusted when your bird is flying loose in the house. It is a natural reaction for a dog or a cat to give chase to a bird that it feels it can catch. If your parakeet has had its wings cut, so much more the danger.

Birds have been blinded by the sharp tooth of a cat. They have had their wings broken, their legs dislocated. But the major cause of death after being attacked by another pet is internal injuries. These are the ones that are hard to detect. There seems to be no outward sign of injury, yet the bird is listless and refuses to eat. In a few days it dies.

Other accidents occur when the bird perches on door tops and someone enters the room and closes the door not suspecting the bird to be there. More than one budgie has lost his beak when it was caught in the door.

Parakeets are attracted to running water. It is their curious nature and their investigative personality. Never run hot water into a sink or basin when your bird is free in the house. It may fly over to investigate and fall into the scalding water.

Facing Page: It is not hard for you to provide your bird with sound health throughout its life.

Always be sure doors and windows are securely closed before releasing your budgie. He will be quickly attracted to an open window and fly out and away before you can stop him. Parakeets become almost entranced by freedom and will fly straight up and away. Seldom has one ever flown into a nearby tree where it could readily be captured, and fewer still have returned to the window from which they escaped.

Other sources of danger for your bird are electric heaters, hair dryers, and frayed electrical cords. Your parakeet will love to pick at anything he can unravel, and he will pick constantly at a frayed cord. Curtains are a delight to the bird, so if you allow your bird the freedom of the house, be sure the curtains he perches on are inexpensive and washable. Not only will he pick holes in them, but out of necessity you will have to launder the curtains occasionally.

BROKEN WINGS AND LEGS: The most frequent injuries to birds are broken legs and broken wings. The leg of a parakeet is very fragile and easily broken. In most cases it will heal without attention, but the bird will be permanently crippled. Even so, he will learn to get around quite adequately with the use of his beak and one good leg.

It is a simple matter to splint the leg. If you decide to try setting the leg and splinting it yourself, select a suitable material for a splint such as a flat toothpick, match'stick, or a piece of plastic that has been heated and shaped to the bird's leg. With one person holding the bird, and a second person doing the splinting, use the healthy leg as a pattern. Be sure the toes are pointing in the normal direction then wrap with a bandage so that the splint is secure, but not so tight as to cut off the circulation of blood in the leg. You may prefer to have your veterinarian perform this task. Healing requires roughly two weeks.

Broken wings are easily bound by placing a piece of gauze pad between the wing and the bird's body. Then securely wrap and fasten the bird's wing against its body with a strip of gauze. Wrap with enough turns to hold the wing securely in place, and also enough so that if he picks at the gauze it will not unravel or loosen. Fasten with adhesive tape. Do not allow the bird out of its cage until the healing is complete to

prevent it from attempting to use its flight muscles. Healing of a broken wing takes two to three weeks.

CLAWS AND BEAKS: Claws and beaks continue to grow, and in the caged bird the overgrowth of the claw can become a problem. It is a simple matter to clip the toenails with a nail clipper as long as you are careful not to cut into the blood vessel in the nail. Should some bleeding occur, the application of styptic powder will stop the flow of blood.

The beak is another matter. As long as a cuttlebone is supplied to help file the beak as it grows, there should not be a problem with an overgrown beak. If the beak does grow too long it can cause problems in eating, making it difficult for the budgie to pick up seeds and shell them. When a bird does develop a beak that requires clipping, it can be trimmed to its normal length with a pair of dog toenail clippers.

COLDS: Colds occur when birds are kept in drafty quarters or where the temperature is allowed to drop at night and rise during the day. The biggest hazard to birds is drafts, either hot or cold. A bird with a cold will sit with its eyes closed

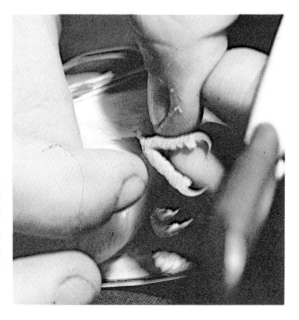

The claws of the budgerigar must be maintained. Clipping the toenails is a simple matter but should be proceeded upon with care; have someone aid you if you are uncertain.

for a long period of time. Upon examination, the eyes appear to be watery and light sensitive. Apply a sterile eye ointment with the tip of a clean finger or a cotton swab. This should be reapplied daily until the condition clears. Antibiotics for treating mild infections that have cold symptoms are available for adding to the drinking water.

CONSTIPATION: Constipation is evident when the bird picks at the vent region with his beak and there is a lack of droppings in the cage. A change of diet is recommended. To give immediate relief administer a small dose of a safe laxative with an eye dropper.

CUTS AND WOUNDS: Cuts and wounds can be treated with hydrogen peroxide to clean them. If they are deep, apply an antibiotic ointment.

DIARRHEA: Diarrhea is another indication of poor diet. It may also be a sign of unclean water or contaminated food. Correcting the diet will usually clear up the diarrhea. In the event that the diarrhea is caused by an infection, add a small amount of antibiotic to the drinking water. Vitamin B12

All birds require gravel to digest their food properly. There are different sizes of gravel available for the different sized birds. Some parakeet gravels, such as the Hagen Products gravel shown here, contain other dietary essentials as well.

may be added to the water, but not in combination with the antibiotic. Add four drops per two ounces of water and continue this treatment until the droppings have returned to normal.

EGG BINDING: This condition occurs occasionally in females. If the condition is corrected in time, an egg-bound female will pass the egg without ill effect. If untreated it prevents the passing of droppings and can cause toxemia and subsequent death to the bird. Egg binding occurs when the egg is not expelled from the body and lodges in the cloaca or lower

Living World offers an array of food supplements. A different variety can be fed every day to give your bird a varied diet.

oviduct. Effectively treating the condition requires two persons: one to hold the bird with the belly up while a second person applies several drops of lukewarm mineral oil into the vent with an eye dropper. After this treatment the bird should be returned to her cage and left undisturbed. In most cases she will pass the egg within a few hours.

FORCE FEEDING: If your bird will not drink or eat, a medicine dropper can be used to force-feed him. Give one drop

at a time so as not to choke him. Place the tip of the dropper in the side of the mouth and gently squeeze the dropper bulb. Use caution so that you do not force air into the bird by being sure the solution is at the tip of the dropper and not in the bulb.

Sick birds that do not eat can be fed this way with a solution of honey and water. The bird will require roughly ten drops of the mixture per day.

HEAT STROKE: Heat stroke occurs when the bird's cage is left in a location where there is no protection from the sun. It often happens when a person places the cage in a shady area out of doors or indoors near a window. With the passage of time, the sun moves so that it hits the cage directly. If a concrete or white surface is near, the intensity of the sun's rays are reflected with many more times their brilliance causing heat stroke in a very short period of time. Birds that suffer from heat stroke usually do not recover unless the condition is caught in time. Bring the bird immediately into the house and attempt to bring the body temperature down by sprinkling it lightly with cool (never cold) water.

The use of a proper net will help prevent injuries when retrieving a budgie.

This magnificently healthy bird presents a penetratingly confident and proud look sure to catch the eye of any onlooker. The amount of time and money necessary to raise a budgie is not great, yet the rewards are, especially if you raise such a one as this.

LICE AND MITES: Lice and mites are parasites that live in cracks and crevices of cages. They get into the corners, under the paper lining the bottom, into nicks in the perches. These are blood-sucking parasites and if left untreated can lead to anemia of the bird.

Although the insects are extremely tiny, they can be seen with the naked eye. Sometimes they are seen crawling over the bird, or when inspected at close range can be seen

A periodic and thorough inspection of your bird, including its underbelly, allows you to spot health problems before it's too late.

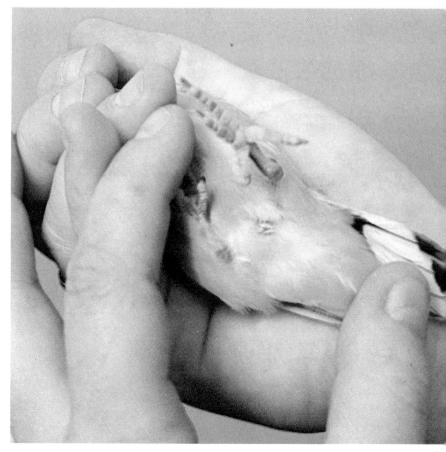

Look carefully for signs of illness when selecting your budgie.

crawling under the feathers against the skin. These parasites cause the parakeet to scratch and peck at his feathers frequently.

Lice and mites can be eliminated with commercial preparations available at pet shops. There are liquids and sprays that can be applied on a weekly basis, but unless a new bird is introduced, once the problem is solved it should not be necessary to continue the treatment.

WATERY EYES: Watery eyes can either be conjunctivitis or the symptom of another disorder such as a cold. Conjunctivitis can be treated with the application of an antibiotic eye ointment. If you suspect a cold or some other ailment, add an antibiotic to the drinking water.

Many ailments can be treated with either aureomycin or streptomycin. These can be purchased from a veterinary supply or a pet shop. A small amount of the antibiotic is mixed with the drinking water, and no other water is offered until all the medicated mixture has been consumed. Treatment should continue for 24 hours after all symptoms have passed.

BREEDING

If by now you have enjoyed your bird so much that you have decided to purchase a mate of the opposite sex and try your hand at breeding, you are among the many who are on the road to becoming an aviculturist. Through selective breeding, parakeet breeders have successfully produced a variety of colors that make breeding an interesting challenge and a rewarding hobby.

There are only a few essentials required to breeding your birds. The first is a nest box. A simple box designed to fit on the outside of the cage, which must be made accesible to the birds, is satisfactory for a beginning or for one or two pairs. This little box fits to the outside of a regular size cage and allows easy access for both the male and female to enter the box and sit on the eggs and care for the young.

Normal household temperatures are quite satisfactory for breeding parakeets. However, if you are contemplating going into breeding on a large scale and plan to build an outdoor aviary, it must be heated in the winter if you are in any but the warmest of climates. In Arizona, parakeet breeders breed out-of-doors in the spring, summer and fall months. In this warm climate, during the winter the birds are housed in unheated quarters, but they do not breed. To prevent the birds from mating during a warm spell and then having the chicks die during a cold spell, the nest boxes are removed from the aviary.

With controlled temperature, the birds will breed year 'round, producing four to five clutches of eggs.

Before breeding the pair, bring them into condition with the addition of good green foods. Also, continue the feeding of greens during the period of time the birds are raising and feeding the young. In the wild, the parakeets breed only when

Facing Page: Here a parent is watching over its newly hatched chicks. A parakeet's average brood is five chicks; in this photo, two are visible.

Three recently hatched chicks are trying to keep warm.

there is an abundance of green food available. The addition of greens is supplying what nature would supply.

The addition of a mineral supplement or a high quality wheat germ oil or a commercial nesting food is beneficial for breeding birds.

Since the production of a strong egg shell and the development of strong bones in the young depend upon the amount of calcium the female bird receives, add generous amounts of cuttlebone, calcium block, oyster shell and grit.

An aid to breeding in an aviary is a piece of whole wheat bread dotted with wheat germ oil and placed where all

Once they are hatched, chicks will grow rapidly.

The cuttlebone is used by the budgie to properly maintain its beak; it is also a good source of calcium, a trace element especially necessary for breeding mothers to insure strong egg and bone development.

the birds in the colony can feed on it. Fresh vegetables can be fed freely to maintain normal bowel movements. Should the bowels become hard and difficult to pass, add a little lime water (two or three drops) to the drinking water.

When the birds are bred out-of-doors in the summer and temperatures rise, they become uncomfortable and there is more chance of the eggs breaking within the nest as the parent birds move about more. Also, mites may be more prevalent in the outdoor aviary than indoors and more prevalent in the summer than in winter. If the birds become too warm, or disturbed by mites, they may desert the eggs.

The breeder must weigh the benefits of outdoor breeding against the benefits of indoor breeding. The main consideration with indoor breeding is space. If one is breeding only one or two pairs, space is of no consequence; but when the hobbyist decides to raise many birds, he needs all the space possible.

Breeding parakeets should be given all the exercise and flight room it is possible to provide, as they spend many hours on the nest during incubation of the eggs and they ap-

These young have similar markings; one is still quite immature.

preciate the opportunity to fly when off the nest. Also, the high caloric content of the breeding ration, along with the hours spent on the nest, tends to let the birds get overly fat if they cannot fly.

The nest box should have a 3½-inch round hole in the center and a perch outside to make access easy. Material should be placed on the floor of the box to provide a cushion for the eggs. It can be shavings, dry grass from the lawn, oatmeal, or other like materials. They will arrange it to their liking,

Nest boxes made of cardboard may be used in a pinch, but the wooden types sold in pet shops are much more serviceable.

These three chicks all have individual coloration; to an alert eye they can be distinguished almost immediately after hatching.

and if the material is placed inside the box for them, a small amount of dried grass or straw may be placed on the floor of the cage so that the parakeets can carry bits into the box as they attempt nest building.

Copulation between the male and the female will continue daily until the first egg is laid. Two or three days before the first egg is laid, the female may exhibit signs of pregnancy. On the underside of her tail, near the vent, a lump will appear. The male will continue his lovemaking, and the act of copulation will take longer, but the female is uninterested. She spends

Here a mother is seen feeding her young in a natural environment. Such nests can often attract such pests as lice and mites and should not be used by a pet owner or hobbyist.

much of her time in the box arranging the material for her eggs. She appears somewhat bloated and ruffles herself regularly, assuming a hunched position on the perch.

On the days that the eggs are laid, both male and female remain in the box together. As soon as the egg is laid, the female will roll it to the center of the box and tuck it under her breast. Then the incubation begins. When the female comes

This beautiful opaline-light green cock, with its intense coloration, is an imposing sight sure to make itself known in the show world.

out of the box, she should visit the grit cup and calcium block. After the first egg is laid, the pair take turns sitting. The male will take his turn sitting on the eggs during the daylight hours. Only occasionally will the female relieve him during his daily sitting, so that he might eat or drink.

It is the female's responsibility to sit on the eggs at night. The male remains near, locating himself near the box entrance as if to give some protection to his mate within. The female will continue to lay an egg every day until her clutch is complete. The number of eggs varies from four to eight.

The incubation period is 18 days, and the parents continue to sit tightly during the first week after the eggs hatch. When the chicks hatch they appear almost naked, but are actually covered with a sparse yellow down that shows itself as the chicks dry. The chicks are very helpless and blind, and when held in the hand the weight is barely perceptible.

By one week of age they are beginning to develop contour feathers. These first feathers make their appearance in the form of prickly quills. Very gradually the quills unfold to reveal juvenile plumage, and the variety of colors can be noted.

Throughout their development, the chicks are cared for by both parents. During the feeding process, the parent bird will firmly grasp the beak of the chick with its own beak and very vigorously shake its head up' and down. This aids in the movement of regurgitated food from the crop of the parent to the crop of the chick.

The chicks will leave the nest sometime between four and five weeks of age. Within a few hours they are very apt flyers, sometimes successfully flying for some distance on the first attempt. Once they leave the nest, they do not return. The parents will continue to feed the chicks until they begin to show an interest in seed and grass. They rapidly learn to hull their own seeds, and at this point they are ready to be weaned and hand tamed.

IN CLOSING

You have selected an exciting and companionable pet in purchasing a parakeet. Whether or not you decide to breed your bird, or teach it to talk, it will give you many years of enjoyment. Birds are naturally clean creatures and require little in the way of care and feeding. They make no demands upon their owners, only that they be given a little companionship and be maintained in a healthy condition.

Birds are remarkable creatures in that they communicate with both body language and sounds. The author has a ring-necked dove that has developed an attraction for cats. Whenever a cat enters the room, the dove hops down from his perch and begins a routine courtship and cooing performance.

The personalities of birds are as varied as those of bird fanciers. In selecting a young bird, you have the opportunity to develop that personality to your own peculiarities. The bond that develops between yourself and your parakeet will be a memorable one for years to come.

Anyone can enjoy the companionship of a budgie. In apartments where other pets are not permitted, the budgie is a welcome companion. It teaches children the responsibility of caring for a pet; it takes the loneliness away from the elderly. Wherever there is a small niche large enough to hold a bird cage, the budgie will find a home.

FACING PAGE: We cast a closing glance at a group of young budgies. Budgerigars are wonderful pets capable of mastering many feats, and their breeding ability makes possible a rewarding hobby.

The following books by T.F.H. publications are available at pet shops everywhere.

ADVENTURES WITH TALKING BIRDS
By Katherine Hurlbutt
ISBN 0-8766-895-3
TFH H-1029
Audience: An anecdotal approach to learning about the behavior and abilities of birds. The insights which the author shares were gained over a period of fifteen years and included experiences with such birds as budgies, cockatiels, cockatoos, ravens, starlings and mynahs.
Hardcover, 5⅜ x 8, 288 pages
64 color photos, many black and white photos.

SUGGESTED READING

THE COMPLETE CAGE AND AVIARY BIRD HANDBOOK
By David Alderton
ISBN 0-86622-113-1
T.F.H. H-1087
Contents: Avian Origins and Features; The Pet Bird; Housing Guidelines; Feeding Guidelines; Management Guidelines; Avian Ailments; Breeding and Colour; The Breeds and Species.
Audience: Author David Alderton, well-known for his books and articles on avicultural subjects, examines the whole field of cage and aviary birds. Treating the species by family, he provides current up-to-date information on both the popular species and many of the less commonly seen birds as well. Highlighted with more than 240 illustrations (almost 175 in full-color) that help the reader to identify the species and varieties along with excellently detailed illustrations showing the design of aviaries and furnishings.
Hard cover, 7½ x 9½", 160 pages.
167 full-color photos accompanied by 20 black and white photographs and more than 60 drawings.

SUGGESTED READING

THE COMPLETE BIRDS OF THE WORLD (ILLUSTRATED EDITION)
By Michael Walters
ISBN 0-87666-894-5
TFH H-1022

This book lists every bird species in the world and gives for each the family relationship range, common and scientific names and related important data. Birds of 120 different families are shown in beautiful (and mostly large) full-color photos; there are more than 550 full-color illustrations in total. This magnificent volume enables bird watchers, aviculturists, dealers and scientists to learn the distribution, habitat, feeding and nesting habits, clutch size, incubation and fledgling period of every family of birds in existence. Written by one of the world's foremost bird authorities and illustrated with some of the finest natural history photographs ever published, this immensely colorful and useful book will be referred to for years regardless of where in the world the reader may live. The book is fully indexed with both common and scientific names for ease of reference. A treasure to own and a pleasure to show, it is one of the finest ornithological works ever produced.

Hard cover, 8½ x 11", 704 pages.
563 color illustrations (mostly large photos)

PARAKEETS OF THE WORLD
By Dr. Matthew M. Vriends
ISBN 0-87666-999-2
TFH H-101

Contents: Buying Parakeets. Care and Maintenance. Cages and Aviaries. Feeding Parakeets. Health and Disease. Description of the Species.

Audience: This book will be useful to both the bird fancier and the professional biologist/ornithologist. It covers only parakeets and small parrots as these are more often kept as pets than the larger parrots. The many color photographs illustrate the majority of the birds.

Hard cover, 5½ x 8½", 352 pp.
224 full-color photos, 115 black and white photos.

Index